Life on Surtsey

www.harpercollinschildrens.com

Book design by Yay! Design
Map and spot illustrations by Sarah Green
The text type was set in Brioso.
The display type was set in Avante Garde Gothic.

The Library of Congress has cataloged the hardcover edition as follows:
Names: Burns, Loree Griffin, author.
Title: Life on Surtsey, Iceland's upstart island / by Loree Griffin Burns.
Other titles: Scientists in the field.
Description: Boston ; New York : Houghton Mifflin Harcourt, [2017] | Series:
Scientists in the field | Audience: Ages 10–12. | Audience: Grades 4 to 6. |
Includes bibliographical references and index.
Identifiers: LCCN 2016042892
Subjects: LCSH: Island ecology—Iceland—Surtsey—Juvenile literature. |
Surtsey (Iceland)—Juvenile literature.
Classification: LCC QH166 .B87 2017 | DDC 577.5/2094912—dc23
LC record available at https://lccn.loc.gov/2016042892

ISBN: 978-0-544-68723-3 hardcover
ISBN: 978-0-358-34823-8 paperback

Printed in the United States of America
PHX 10 9 8 7 6 5 4

More thrilling nonfiction from Loree Griffin Burns

Tracking Trash: Flotsam, Jetsam, and the Science of Ocean Motion

The Hive Detectives: Chronicle of a Honey Bee Catastrophe

Beetle Busters: A Rogue Insect and the People Who Track It

Life on Surtsey

ICELAND'S UPSTART ISLAND

Loree Griffin Burns

Clarion Books
Boston   New York

To Jane Dutton, and to everyone who loved her.

Contents

A Note About Language
An in-depth exploration of the Icelandic language is beyond the scope of this book, but I've tried to include a small taste of its beauty in these pages. The names of Icelandic scientists and Icelandic locations have been spelled using the Icelandic alphabet, and you can find details about unique letters and their pronunciations on page 66. In the Source Notes and Bibliography I've reverted to the Anglicized spellings of these names and places.

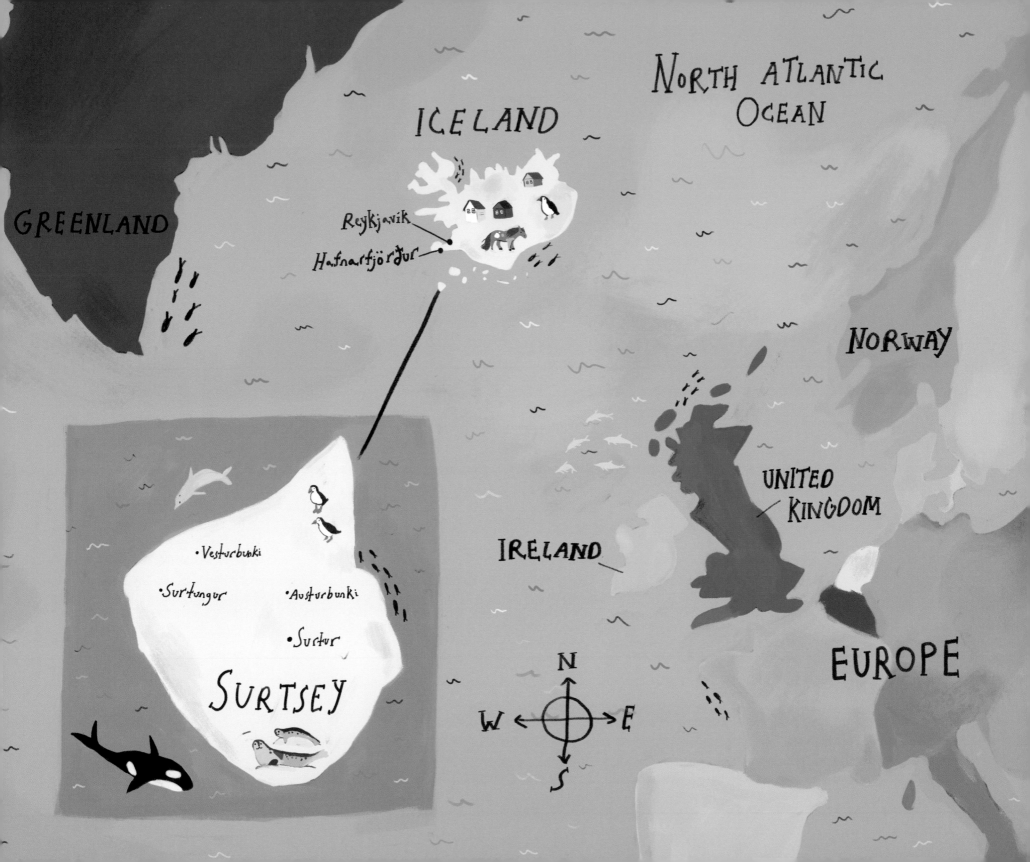

arrival

Drengur Ólafsson was born on September 28, 1949, in Reykjavík, Iceland. Icelanders have a long and proud history of naming their children, and it's probably different from the system you're used to. Icelandic parents, for example, don't give their babies a first name right away. *Drengur* simply means "little boy." Little Boy Ólafsson didn't get his true first name until his parents got to know him a bit. When they did, they called him Erling.

Young Erling reading with his mother.

Facing page: Iceland is an island nation located in the Atlantic Ocean, between northern Europe and Greenland. Surtsey (inset) is part of the Westman Islands, an archipelago extending off the southern coast of the country; it is the farthest island from the mainland.

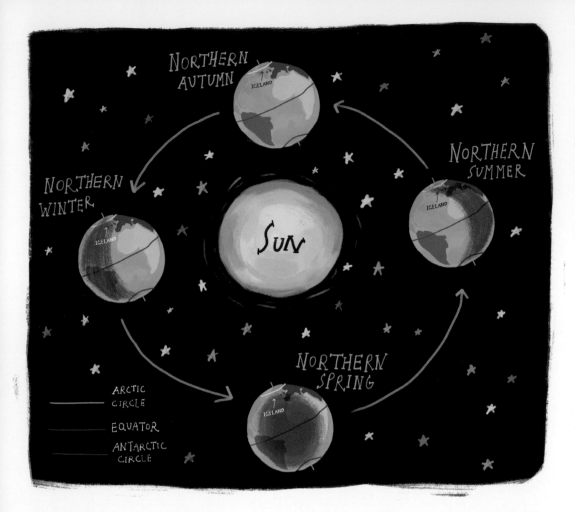

This illustration shows the Earth at four different points on its annual orbit around the sun. Because the planet is tilted, the sun's warming rays strike different parts of it at different angles, which leads to the seasonal fluctuations we know as spring, summer, fall, and winter. For more explanation, see page 67.

Erling and his siblings—three brothers and two sisters—grew up in the city of Hafnarfjörður (pronounced HAFF-nar-fyor-thur), just outside the Icelandic capital. Childhood here is like childhood anywhere: kids go to school, do homework, play on sports teams, explore outside. Iceland as a homeland, however, is unique.

For one thing, the country sits on the edge of the Arctic Circle. That means it's cool. The average temperature in this region during the summer is only 50°F (10°C), and more than ten percent of the country is covered by glaciers. The Arctic Circle also marks the line on the planet at which the amount of sunlight in a given day is significantly altered because of the way the earth tilts on its axis. In the winter, when the Arctic Circle is tilted away from the sun, Icelanders barely see it during the day. The sun rises at lunchtime and sets again well before dinner. In summer, when the Arctic Circle is pointed *toward* the sun, the situation is reversed: the sun rises very early—about three o'clock in the morning—and doesn't set again until the following midnight.

As if all of this weren't strange enough, Iceland also happens to sit on top of an undersea mountain range called the Mid-Atlantic Ridge. This ridge marks the place where two separate, massive plates of the earth's crust are moving away from each other. This movement is extremely slow—only millimeters over the course of a year—but it has some pretty spectacular consequences: namely, volcanoes. Iceland is home to more volcanoes than any other country in the world, and major eruptions happen every five years or so.

Glaciers, summer days that last twenty hours, winter nights that last just as long, and regular volcanic eruptions may sound extreme to you and me, but to the average Icelander, it's all pretty humdrum.

"When not doing homework, we kids stayed outside all the time, in all weather," says Erling. "Ball games, chasing games, hiding games, building snow houses, making wars with snowballs, and sledding were popular. And the lava was our playground, a good landscape, with caves to hide in."

For the people who live in Iceland and the kids who grow up here, ice and fire just aren't that unusual.

But on November 14, 1963, when Erling was fourteen years old, an epically unusual event did shake the country of Iceland. A volcano located fifteen miles off the southern coast exploded under the sea—and gave birth to an island.

The newest earth on Earth arrived with no warning. The area around it was dotted with ancient islands that were known to be volcanic in origin, but it had been six thousand years or more since the last eruption here. When ash and rock and cinder began to spew violently up from the sea, creating a plume of smoke eight times taller than the Empire State Building, all Iceland watched in mild surprise. As these materials settled back down into the sea, however, the base of the volcano grew wider on the ocean floor . . . and its top grew taller. Eventually that top pushed right up and out of the ocean. By the morning of November 15, pilots flying over the area could see land where none had existed before.

The eruption became international news. Like most people on the planet, Erling read about it in his local paper. Unlike most people, he could actually take in the drama from his house. The eruption cloud eventually stretched high enough to be seen in the town of Hafnarfjörður, and Erling watched it from his bathroom window.

To get a sense of the size and scale of the eruption, note the fishing boat in the foreground of the photo on the left, which was taken on November 19, 1963. One month later, a small but expanding island was clearly visible, as seen in the photo below. Other islands in the Westman archipelago can be seen in the background of this second image.

The eruption that formed Surtsey was both violent and beautiful. In this image, captured on December 1, 1963, lightning scorches the sky above the island.

"I could see smoke over the mountains to the southeast. I would stand by that window for long periods of time, watching nothing happening. It was just a stable smoke column, with no movement," Erling remembers. "But there was something about it."

Witnesses closer to the volcano and the new island reported that the eruptions were violent but made little noise. That's because seawater was constantly flooding the volcano's crater, cooling its molten, or liquified, insides and muffling its angry explosions. An endless spray of lava bombs—solidifying lumps of lava thrown up from the heart of the volcano—rained down over the area, however, punctuating the strange quiet with sizzling saltwater splashes.

"When darkness fell," wrote one observer, "the entire cone glowed with bombs, which rolled down the slopes into the white surf. Lightning ripped the eruption cloud with purplish bolts, and thunder cracked above our heads."

The volcano was eventually named for the Icelandic god of fire, Surtur. The island it produced was called Surtsey (SURTS-ay), which means "Surtur's island" in Icelandic. Over the next three years, additional vents opened in the undersea ridge around Surtsey. Each new volcano spewed more ash, cinder, rock, and steam. Twice more, islands were formed, but they were tiny compared with Surtsey, and the sea quickly swallowed them again.

Young volcanic islands, being piles of ash and cinder and rock (geologists call the mix *tephra*) are quite fragile. Tephra is easily lifted up into the wind and carried away, and what isn't blown away is washed away by waves.

If, however, a volcanic island grows large enough, and if its volcano keeps supplying more and more tephra, it can survive the waves and the wind. This is what happened with Surtsey. The volcano spewed ash and cinder and rocks, which built the island up. The Atlantic threw waves of seawater that washed the island away. Surtur responded with still more tephra.

Scientists watched this battle closely. When a second volcano belched to life—adding even more ash, cinder, and rock—the island grew more quickly. Surtsey was soon so big that waves couldn't reach the craters of Surtur or the new volcano, Surtungur. No longer muffled by the sea, the eruptions grew loud. At the same time, the two volcanic craters began to fill with molten lava.

In April 1964, five months after the initial eruption, molten lava pushed up and over the crater walls for the first time, slowly flowing down the outside of those walls and blanketing the southern part of the island.

"Those of us who witnessed the scene from the air could hardly contain our fascination," wrote one Icelandic geologist. "We had never before seen a fountain of such ravishing beauty—and now the future of the island was ensured."

Ensured because—unlike delicate tephra—lava, when cooled, hardens into a solid rocklike substance that is much more resistant to the pounding of ocean waves. As the southern end of Surtsey was coated in lava, the tephra foundation beneath was protected. The island would survive, at least for a while.

From the moment its shores popped out of the sea, people were drawn to Surtsey. When the island was only three months old and still erupting, a team of scientists and reporters made one of the earliest landings. They arrived in a large ship, which was anchored offshore while the team set out for Surtsey in inflatable rubber boats called dinghies. The sea was rough, and the dinghies capsized. Cameras and other equipment were lost forever and, in the words of one of the scientists, "everyone got a ducking." Believe it or not, that was the easy part of their trip.

"Hardly were we ashore," one of them later wrote, "when Surtur fired a barrage of warning shots. Clouds of black ash billowed against the sky, and bombs rained down on the slopes of the crater. Just off our beach, falling bombs of lava and pumice caused geyser-like splashes in the sea, and now the missiles began to crash into the sand around us. It took a strong effort of will to stand still and stare skyward to watch the trajectory of the bombs. The trick was not to dodge them until the last moment before they seemed about to land on our heads."

All seven members of the team made it back to their ship alive.

By April 1964, Surtsey was fully formed and its two volcanic craters clearly visible: Surtungur is to the west (left in this image) and Surtur, still erupting, is to the east. In the foreground is the island Jólnir, which washed back into the sea shortly after it formed.

In June 1967, after three years and seven months of near-constant eruption, the volcanoes on Surtsey fell silent. The island was by then about the size of New York City's Central Park, and more attractive than ever to would-be adventurers. But Icelandic scientists, in conjunction with the country's government, worked to have the island protected. Surtsey was declared a nature preserve, and off-limits to all tourists. Scientists alone were given permission to explore it.

What would scientists do on Surtsey? Lots. But the main opportunity would be simply to watch this giant lump of sterile tephra and lava change over time. When the eruption ended, the island was lifeless. There were no plants, no animals, no visible living creatures of any sort. Scientists knew this was temporary. Already seaweed had begun to wash ashore on the island, and birds had been seen visiting.

"A volcanic island newly emerged from the ocean is completely devoid of life," wrote the geologist and early Surtsey explorer Sigurður Þorarinsson. "When, how, from where, and in what order does life invade such an island?"

Sigurður and his colleagues intended to find out. When the lava bombs stopped dropping from the sky, he and other scientists visited the island. Their records of these early trips read like adventure novels.

"There were cracking noises when the newly congealed surface of the lava crust gave way below one's feet and red-hot magma could be seen glowing in the crevices," wrote the biologist Sturla Friðriksson. (For the record, Sturla's colleagues measured the temperature of that magma, which is molten lava flowing underground instead of above it. The temperature was more than 2,000°F. As a comparison, the oven in your kitchen only goes up to 500°F!) "It was not advisable to remain long in the same spot, for the soles of one's boots soon started to smolder, and if a rucksack was carelessly left behind it might start to melt in the uprush of hot air."

None of this deterred future scientists.

By the time of the first formal post-eruption expedition in 1967, Erling was in high school and thinking about a career in science. He planned to continue his studies at the University of Iceland. He didn't know it yet, but he'd soon burn his own boots on the shores of the island he'd watched from the bathroom window of his childhood home.

In April 1964, lava began to flow from the volcanic craters on Surtsey.

Sizing Up Surtsey

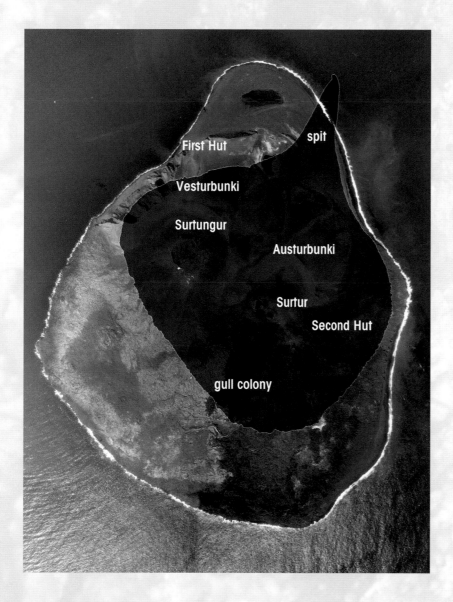

First Hut

spit

Vesturbunki

Surtungur

Austurbunki

Surtur

Second Hut

gull colony

When the eruption that formed Surtsey ended in June of 1967, the island was approximately one square mile (2.6 square kilometers) in size and 571 feet (174 meters) tall at its highest point. Forty-five years later, the island had eroded to half that size (0.5 square miles, or 1.3 square kilometers) and only 509 feet (155 meters) above sea level at its highest point. The schematic shown here, created by overlaying aerial photographs taken in 1967 (black and white) and 2014 (red), show this change dramatically. Note the location of the first research hut built on the island. Scientists predict the island will survive for hundreds of years, but not for thousands.

The first research hut built on Surtsey, shown here, stood for twenty years before erosion of the island forced the construction of a newer hut on higher ground.

life

Since I was a tiny kid, I've always been wild," says Erling. "My parents knew from the beginning where I was headed."

Which isn't to say that his parents knew Erling would end up living on an uninhabited volcanic island; it's just that they knew their son was passionate about the natural world from the start. As a child, he pored over every page of every volume in the collection of Danish animal books his grandmother loaned him. His first language was Icelandic, of course, but he taught himself to read Danish in order to know what these books had to say about the lions and tigers drawn on their pages.

The set of animal books that belonged to Erling's grandmother now belong to him. The Danish title *Averdens dyr* means "The whole world's animals" in English.

As he got older, Erling became interested in birds, spending his free time scouring Hafnarfjörður for the migrant species that sometimes stop in Iceland. He kept notebooks detailing these exploits, eventually sharing them with the most famous bird scientist in all of Iceland.

Later, around the time Surtsey was exploding out of the sea, Erling had a Danish pen pal who collected insects. The moment Erling saw this friend's pinned insect collection, he said to himself, *Ah, this is for me*. He began to study insects and pinned a collection of his own.

Erling puts it this way: "I'm interested in everything that breathes."

In 1969, twenty-year-old Erling began a formal study of everything that breathes by majoring in biology—the study of living things—at the University of Iceland. By this time, scientists had been making regular expeditions to Surtsey for several years. A hut had been built on the island, and researchers monitoring the arrival of plants and animals could now visit for days at a time.

How would organisms reach Surtsey?

Which ones would arrive first?

Would they establish themselves permanently?

Before Surtsey, scientists had had few chances to study a sterile island. Perhaps the best had been in Indonesia, on the island of Krakatoa (sometimes spelled *Krakatau*), where modern history's "greatest, wildest, loudest, and most lethal volcano" let loose in 1883. The eruption killed forty thousand people and, shockingly, completely obliterated the island itself. But several decades later, in 1927, an eruption in the same volcanic system formed a new island. Anak Krakatoa, which means "child of Krakatoa," rose up from the ashes of the original island over the course of several years. Eventually, conditions on Anak Krakatoa were similar to what scientists would years later find on the newly formed shores of Surtsey: the island was about the same size, about the same height, about the same age, and about the same distance from other land forms. Unfortunately, scientists didn't begin studying the arrival of plants and animals on Anak Krakatoa right away. And as the climate there is warm and tropical, the establishment of plant and animal life happened *very* quickly. To complicate matters even further, tourists from surrounding islands and elsewhere regularly visited Anak Krakatoa, leaving behind everything from trash to stowaway insects. These were not easy conditions in which to carefully study how a brand-new island becomes a home to living things.

In contrast, because of Surtsey's harsh Arctic climate, plants and animals establish themselves more slowly there. A plant that manages to take root in the summertime, for example, will have to survive an Arctic winter in an exposed place in order to bloom again the following summer. Also, thanks to its designation as a nature preserve, Surtsey is protected from visiting tourists. The organisms that make it to the island are likely to have arrived on their own, by natural means. Because of these advantages, Surtsey should give scientists a slower-motion view of succession and ecosystem formation. Here scientists will be able to watch living communities slowly develop from scratch.

But the very same conditions that foster this slow colonization on Surtsey also make it a difficult place to conduct field research. Trips to the island are all but impossible in the winter, when storms and high seas in the area prevent boats and planes from reaching it safely. And in the calmer summer months, the danger and expense of transporting scientists and all their supplies to an island with very few spots to land a boat made early monitoring of the island difficult.

Around the time Erling graduated from college, the organizing body for scientific research on the island, the Surtsey Research Society, decided to station field researchers there for the entire summer. They built a permanent hut so that instead of traveling back and forth to the mainland, researchers could live on Surtsey for months at a time, studying all aspects of the island's development without interruption. In order for this plan

Seagulls, like this pair of lesser black-backed gulls (*Larus fuscus*), arrived on Surtsey early and under their own power.

to work, though, the society needed to find someone who knew a lot about the plants, animals, and insects that might make their way to the island. They needed someone who was a fastidious observer and conscientious note keeper, someone who wouldn't mind living on an uninhabited and barely cooled-off volcanic island in the Arctic Circle for a three-month stretch.

Erling got the job.

"It was not easy to fall asleep the night after the idea was first proposed to me," he remembers. Not because he was nervous, mind you, but because he was ecstatic.

"One of my professors offered me another job, as a field assistant on the island of Jan Mayen, north of Iceland. It was very tempting, but the choice was easy. Surtsey. Wow."

And so on June 15, 1970, Erling and three other young men—two to carry out plant studies and one to serve as their cook and communications specialist—set out on a small fishing boat, towing a rubber dinghy. Several hours later they were standing on the shores of Surtsey, gear and dinghy piled around, watching the fishing boat head back to the mainland without them.

"I don't have words to describe it," Erling says, "standing there on the shore for the first time."

Remembering that day, when he first stood on a chunk of lava that few humans had stood on before, an island he would come to know as well as anyone else on Earth, he eventually finds a single word that works.

"Home."

"The first visitation of life on Surtsey occurred only two weeks after the island had pushed up through the waves," reads a 1965 newspaper article. "It was a seagull."

It wasn't too surprising to see a seagull on Surtsey, because they were known to live and breed on nearby islands. Scientists knew it was only a matter of time before the gulls began breeding on Surtsey, too. They also knew the arrival of birds would change the island in important ways.

First of all, birds would surely bring other life forms with them. Nesting materials flown in from nearby islands might include whole plants or seeds, and either of these could potentially take root in Surtsey's sandy surfaces. Scraps of fish and other meals carried from the sea would eventually rot in that same sand, adding nutrients that would make it an even better growing material for roots and seeds. Bird poop would do the same thing.

But that's not all.

Mites and tiny insects that live in or get stuck on the feathers of birds, or in the plant materials the birds might carry to the island for nesting, would also start to arrive.

Erling was now poised to watch this part of Surtsey's story unfold.

In addition to flying in on their own power or being transported by animals that could fly in on their own power, new life forms could also reach Surtsey by sea. Six months after the eruption started, waterlogged leaves and stems from two different plants were found among the debris washed up on black lava sand of Surtsey's shore. Seeds from three different plants were found too, and when scientists potted them in soil back on the mainland, these seeds grew into plants. Could such seeds ever germinate in the lava sand of Surtsey? If a seed did germinate and produce a plant on the island, could this plant survive a winter on the edge of the Arctic Circle? The key to answering these questions, and to understanding the colonization of a new island, would be patient observation, season after season, year after year.

This tuft of grass, photographed among boulders on the spit in 1972, most likely drifted to Surtsey from a nearby island.

A Lupine Is a Lupine Is a Lupine . . . or Is It?

Scientists have been using a two-name (binomial) system to name and classify organisms since Carl Linnaeus first suggested the idea in 1753. The system uses Latin words to describe the genus and species of an organism, and it helps avoid the confusion that arises when people in far-flung regions of the world call the same organism by different names . . . or different organisms by the same name. For example, *lupine* is what Icelanders call the invasive purple flower that blooms across the country in midsummer. Although a related plant grows in the northeastern United States, and even though gardeners there also call it lupine, the two plants are not the same. The Icelandic plant is *Lupinus nootkatensis,* imported from Alaska, and the New England plant is *Lupinus polyphyllus.* In this book, organisms are mostly identified by the names commonly used in Iceland; in cases where organisms are shown in photographs, both the common name and the Latin binomial are provided in the caption.

And so Erling's main charge that first summer was straightforward: record everything he saw, collect everything he could, add to the record of life's arrival on Surtsey.

"The three of us were out every day, watching and searching for anything special," Erling says. For three months, day in and day out, rain or shine, they made their rounds and took their notes.

"I walked around the island, along the cliffs, along the shore, every single day, counting birds, netting insects, looking for drift on the shore. Occasionally I saw black guillemots passing by or swimming on the surface of the sea."

Black guillemots are sleek black sea birds with distinctive white wing patches and bright orange legs. The inside of their bills is the same shocking orange. Guillemots are common on Heimaey (HAY-ma-ay), the largest of the nearby islands, and scientists were eager to know whether the birds would attempt to breed on Surtsey too.

In the middle of July, Erling began to suspect that they were.

"I saw this pair swimming below the cliffs, giving their peculiar high-frequency alarm sound," he remembers. He thought the alarm call might mean that the birds were protecting something. Such as eggs.

Guillemots often lay eggs on bare rock ledges like those found on Surtsey. Placed midway up a cliff face, the eggs are low enough to provide the parents easy access to food from the ocean, but high enough that waves can't wash the eggs away. Erling became convinced that the pair of guillemots he was watching had laid eggs on Surtsey's cliffs.

"On July 27 I saw one of the guillemots flying toward the cliff with a fish in its bill and disappearing somewhere in the cliffs."

There was only one way to find out for sure. Erling had to investigate the cliff face, which stretched more than forty feet (thirteen meters) above the North Atlantic Ocean.

"I fetched my two fellow botanists—the cook was busy sunbathing! No joke!—and two ropes."

He tied one of the ropes around his waist, giving the free end to his two companions. The second rope was knotted in several places, securely tied to a lava rock on the top of the cliff, and draped down toward the ocean. Erling planned to climb down this second rope, knot to knot, while his companions used all their strength to secure him by the waist with the first rope.

You may think, reading this, that Erling was fearless. He insists this isn't true. He claims to have a healthy fear of heights. Just before lowering himself over the side of the cliff—supported only by a couple of ropes, a couple of young men, and a hunk of lava—he thought about this fear. More specifically, he thought

In addition to recording plant, insect, and bird life, Erling collected daily measurements from the meteorological equipment that had been placed on Surtsey.

An adult black guillemot (*Cepphus grylle*) perched on the lava cliffs of Surtsey.

Two of Surtsey's most famous historical residents: the half-grown guillemot chicks that Erling found hiding in the cliffs during the summer of 1970. This image provided the first and most convincing proof that birds had begun nesting on the island.

about what might happen to him if he fell. But then he simply focused on guillemots and guillemot eggs and nothing else.

"So down I went, and I searched all the cracks I passed."

There were a lot of cracks.

But eventually, in one narrow crevice about twenty feet above the ocean, Erling found more than guillemot eggs. He found two half-grown guillemot chicks!

"I managed to get them out, put them inside my coat, and take them up to the top of the cliff."

With his feet on solid lava sand again, Erling pulled out the chicks, one in each hand, and posed them for his colleagues. The photo they took that day was the first definitive evidence of an animal breeding on Surtsey.

And then?

"Down the cliff face again, to return the chicks to their crack." Erling laughs.

Not long after the guillemot discovery, Erling watched another species of sea bird, northern fulmars, from the rocky beach below the western cliffs of Surtsey. He'd observed these gray and white gulls sitting on the cliff ledges for months, coming and going. He knew that fulmars liked to breed on ledges (not in crevices like the guillemots), but he wasn't sure whether anything special (such as breeding) was going on yet. Then one day he was surprised to see through his binoculars a young fulmar. The bird was too young to have flown to Surtsey.

"This time I climbed up the ledge, not down," Erling remembers.

And in doing so, he found and recorded for the world, for the second time in as many months, a bird species definitively breeding on Surtsey.

An adult northern fulmar (*Fulmarus glacialis*) with chick, photographed on Surtsey.

Another avian resident of Surtsey is the black-legged kittiwake (*Rissa tridactyla*). Check out the white bird droppings spattered on the black lava around the nests—there are a lot of nutrients in that excrement!

"Two nesting species during my first stay on the island," Erling remembers. "It was like scoring a second goal in a winning game. This was something for a kid like me."

At summer's end, Erling left Surtsey more convinced than ever that he would dedicate his professional life to further understanding the flora and fauna of Iceland. He was invited to spend a second summer on Surtsey, and he did. But after that, the funding for summerlong Surtsey expeditions ran out. Instead Erling spent his next two summers on the edge of one of Iceland's great glaciers, studying the insects and spiders that lived in a pink-footed goose colony there. He became more and more excited about field research.

"For four whole summers I was away from what we call civilization," Erling remembers. "And I never missed it."

After graduating from college, Erling moved to Sweden to attend Lund University, where he was formally trained as an entomologist, a scientist who specializes in insect studies. The moment he finished, he returned to Iceland. And to Surtsey.

"I'm very devoted to this island," Erling says. "I love it. And it's a love that never cools."

Erling on Surtsey in the summer of 2015.

Surtsey, as seen from the air.

growth

I t takes a four-bladed twin-engine rescue helicopter two trips to get the 2015 Surtsey expedition—eight scientists and two observers, plus equipment and food for one week—safely to the island. Erling travels with the first group, a camera hanging over his inflatable life vest. Every flight over Surtsey offers him a rare opportunity to photograph (and later, back at home, more closely study) Surtsey's tall lava cliffs and the birds that live there. So before takeoff, Erling reminds the pilot to fly at least one full circle around the island before landing.

Erling photographs Surtsey's perimeter from the air as an Icelandic coast guard officer looks on.

Most years Erling can take the photos he needs through the helicopter window. Today, however, it's raining. Visibility through the small rectangle of glass at the back of the helicopter is terrible. But the crew knows how important flyover images are to Erling's work, so when Surtsey comes into view, one of them waves him forward. (The roar of helicopter blades and engines is much too loud to hear anyone talking.) Erling makes his way to the center of the aircraft, where he is fitted into a harness. Securely tethered, he sits cross-legged on the floor between a pile of gear and the door of the helicopter. He adjusts his baseball cap, tightens his grip on the camera, flashes a thumbs-up to the crewman. The door in front of him slides open, and he lifts his camera and starts to shoot.

Through the open door, everyone onboard can see the birds, the tall black cliffs they call home, the froth of ocean waves smashing into the base of those cliffs, and, when the angle of the helicopter is just right, the entire expanse of the island they are coming to monitor.

Most of Surtsey's edges are sheer cliff faces. In some places these cliffs stretch more than forty feet (thirteen meters, or about as high as a school bus is long) up from the surface of the ocean. Even though they are coated with lava, the pounding of the northern Atlantic challenges these cliffs constantly, reshaping the island one crashing cliff slide at a time. The exception is Surtsey's northern shore, which slopes gradually to a low, rocky beach, a spit of land that points back toward the mainland. Wind and waves change the shape of the spit drastically each winter; this year it looks remarkably like the tiny arm of Massachusetts known as Cape Cod.

Two mountainous ridges rise from the middle and the western edge of the island. These are Austurbunki and Vesturbunki, remnants of tephra cones that built up around the volcanoes that formed Surtsey. (Austurbunki and Vesturbunki mean "eastern cone" and "western cone" in English.) Their surfaces are lighter in color than the rest of the island, and marked with erosion lines. Beside the ridges are the volcanic craters. Surtur, the smaller crater, sits beside Austurbunki; and Surtungur, the larger, sits beside Vesturbunki. Spreading out from the nonridged side of each crater, stretching to the southern and eastern edges of the island, is a large field of black lava. And in the very center of the lava is an unexpected splash of lush green plant life. This is the gull colony, home to hundreds of nesting lesser black-backed gulls, greater black-backed gulls, and herring gulls. Even from a helicopter, one can tell that this oasis is the center of life on Surtsey.

When Erling has finished taking pictures, a crewman closes the helicopter door and the pilot turns toward another speck of color: the red roof of the research hut. He lands gently in the middle of a tiny cement landing pad right next to the hut. Things immediately get busy.

The door slides open again, and passengers hop out, Erling first and then several others. Crewmen toss gear through the door two and three items at a time. The scientists try to keep up, handing each box or bag or suitcase from one person to another until the last in line drops it into the chunky black sand. Within minutes,

An Icelandic coast guard rescue helicopter sits on the landing pad on Surtsey after dropping off the expedition team.

the helicopter is aloft again, this time heading to the nearby island of Heimaey, where the rest of the 2015 Surtsey expedition team is waiting for a lift to the island.

Surtsey is as beautiful as it is otherworldly. In all directions the view is of black sand, deep ebony today because of the rain, and lava rocks in black and rust. Here and there around the lava sculptures are mounds of green plants and tufts of brown grass. The only man-made structure in sight is the research hut. Wisps of steam creep low over the ridge's textured surface, a gentle reminder that the researchers are unpacking at the base of a sleeping volcano.

Everyone on this year's team has worked on Surtsey before, so none of them is distracted by this peculiar landscape. Instead, they haul plastic bins of food, backpacks, sleeping bags, and suitcases from the pile next to the landing pad up onto the porch of the research hut. Erling pulls a long metal pole from underneath the hut and uses it to open the wooden shutters locked over the windows. Matthías (for help with pronunciation, see page 32), an entomology student who has come to monitor insect life with Erling, begins moving luggage

The research hut, located at the base of Austurbunki, has sleeping space for up to ten scientists, small food prep and dining areas, and no bathroom facilities. Rainwater is collected from the roof (blue barrel) and boiled for cooking and cleaning; drinking water is brought in by the expedition team.

and supplies into the hut, and Lovísa, a geologist, helps him. Paweł, a botanist, finds a shovel under the hut and starts digging a hole in the sand near the porch; this makeshift refrigerator will keep the team's perishable foods cool for the week.

Erling and the others finish their moving-in chores just as the second half of the 2015 expedition team arrives: Borgþór, Sigurður, Bjarni, and Kristján are all scientists, and Þórdís is a representative from Iceland's Environment Agency. They too have been to Surtsey before; they unload their gear straightaway, paying little attention to the scenery or the steady drizzle.

Erling and his student, Matthías, set to work within an hour of touching down on Surtsey.

In the early years of the island's life, which were also the early years of Erling's career as a professional entomologist, he came here irregularly. In the decade that followed his first two summers here, he was able to get himself to Surtsey only three times: a day in 1976, a week in 1981, and another day in 1984. He was always convinced, however, that regular sampling of insects was critical to telling Surtsey's life story. He worked constantly to secure funding and a position on Surtsey expeditions. Since 2002 he's managed to spend one week on the island every single summer. And when you have only one workweek—five days in all—to assess all the changes that have taken place on an entire island over the course of a year, you can't let rain deter you. By the time the second team has hauled their gear into the hut, Erling and Matthías have assembled the tools they'll need to start trapping insects. Packs on their backs, nets in their hands, they head out into the wet sand.

When scientists began tracking the various forms of life arriving on Surtsey, it was clear that they needed a system for keeping track of *place* on the island. Geologic features were obvious landmarks—the ridges of Austurbunki and Vesturbunki, for example, and the Surtur and Surtungur craters. Another way scientists keep track of location, however, is by overlaying the island with an imaginary grid, much like the system of latitude and longitude used to pinpoint locations on Planet Earth. This grid allows researchers to keep an accurate record of exactly where they find certain plants or animals.

Thirty of the squares of this imaginary grid have been marked out in the sand on Surtsey with permanent wooden stakes, one pounded into each corner. Scientists monitor different aspects of each of these thirty squares during every expedition: botanists keep track of the plant life in each plot; other scientists record the presence of fungi, or of bird nests, or the nutritional composition of the sand. Erling monitors insect life. Today he and Matthías will begin that work by setting pitfall traps in the heart of each of the thirty 10m-by-10m square plots.

Pitfall traps are used to capture terrestrial insects, those that crawl on land rather than flying over it. The traps are surprisingly simple devices. After photographing an individual square, Erling pulls from his backpack a small plastic cup, a soda bottle of clear liquid, a large plastic lid, a large metal staple, and a spoon. He walks to the approximate center of the square, kneels down, and uses the spoon to dig in the black sand. When he's

Close-up of a pitfall trap.

cleared a hole of the right size, he pushes the plastic cup into it, taking care to set its edges completely level with the surface of the sand. Then he pours a bit of the clear liquid, a preservative called formaldehyde, into the trap. A crawling insect walking on the sand is unlikely to notice the cup. When it steps over the edge, it will fall into the formaldehyde, which will both drown and preserve it. Erling and Matthías will come back at the end of the week to collect the insects trapped in each cup. Later, back in Erling's lab on the mainland, they'll identify each and every insect found in each and every cup.

People often ask Erling if it's necessary to kill insects in order to study them. The question surprises him.

"I never think of it that way," he says. Sampling insects that have made their way to Surtsey gives Erling a crucial glimpse into the process by which an ecosystem—a community of living organisms—forms. And by collecting insects year after year, he can watch these newly formed ecosystems evolve. The simple truth is that these samples cannot be collected, identified, and released in a single week; there are simply too many insects to look at. And so Erling traps them and takes them back to the mainland with him. It can take years to properly identify every insect he collects in the course of a single week.

When a trap cup is placed and filled, Erling makes a canopy with the plastic lid and the metal staple. The canopy sits high enough that it won't interfere with insects walking into the trap, but low enough to keep out the rain. Trap set, canopy in place, Erling walks out of the square, carefully reusing the footprints he made on the way in. At the edge of the square, he takes a second photo. Then he shoulders his pack, grabs his net, and hikes to the next square.

Erling and Matthías work this way for hours, and the setting of the first fifteen pitfall traps brings them around the entire southern half of the island on foot. The early squares are in the sandy terrain of Surtsey's middle, but eventually the two make their way toward the island's southern edge. As they do, the terrain changes. The density of plant material increases gradually, and with every step the scenery looks less volcanic. This is a sign that they're nearing the gull colony.

The colony is just as it looked from the air: green and lush. It's filled with the sights and sounds of hundreds of sea gulls: swooping, squawking birds in flight; standing, squawking birds on the ground; and feathers, fish bones, eggshells, old nests, new nests, eggs, nestlings, debris of all sorts. The gull colony is alive with birds, and plants too. Fescue, a type of grass, covers the ground in thick clumps that completely hide all traces of the lava sand it grows in. Two steps into the drenched plants covering the gull colony, and both scientists are soaked to their knees. They trudge on anyway, locate the next square, and set the next trap.

The important role of sea gulls in the evolution of life on Surtsey has been recorded and analyzed by decades of scientists. Early on, before the gulls began breeding here, this area was covered with the same lava

Erling sets a pitfall trap at the center of one of the thirty 10m-by-10m plots on Surtsey. One of the four wooden stakes marking the plot is visible in this image (bottom right), another is half hidden behind Erling, and the last two are outside the frame of the image. You can see a close-up view of a trap on page 24.

formations and thick black sand that covers the rest of the island. The first plants to root here were the same ones that rooted elsewhere on Surtsey's sandy lava: pioneer species that were able to grow in extreme conditions. Unlike the rest of the island, however, the lava fields were also well situated for species of birds who survive on food from the sea. In 1974, four years after Erling first recorded breeding guillemots and fulmars on the island, a pair of greater black-backed gulls built a nest in a mound of sandwort plant that was growing on a sand-covered lava flat. By 1978 there were six nests; in 2002 there were thirty-five, and today at least a hundred pairs nest in the area. The arrival of the birds changed everything on this part of the island.

Some of the changes were easy to see—the nests themselves, excrement covering the lava and sand around

The view out to sea contains more sand, more rock, more plants . . . and distant islands made of essentially the same materials.

the nests, food scraps littering the area. Harder to see, at first, were the changes these additions made in the lava sand itself. Basically, the gulls were adding nutrients to the sand. Decomposing nest materials, excrement, and food scraps made the sand in the lava field much richer than sand in other parts of the island. And richer sand is easier for plants to grow in.

As the gulls enriched the sand, they were also seeding it with new life. The wisps of plant material they carried in to build nests often included rooted plants. It's possible that some of these wisps took hold. More likely, the birds carried in seeds—hidden in nesting material or in the crevices of their feet and feathers or in their excrement. Because of this, seeds arrived in the lava field much more frequently than anywhere else on the island. They were dropped into soil that was richer than anywhere else, too. The seeds sprouted, and the gull colony became the center of plant life on the island.

The plants that thrived in the early years of the gull colony's existence soon gave way to newer species, including grasses such as fescue. These new grasses also thrived in the rich sand, eventually covering the entire area of the colony. As changes to the plant cover in the gull colony progressed, new insect habitats were created. And when insects made it to the island—flying in on their own power, blown in on strong winds, or carried in by birds—some of them thrived in these new habitats.

Prior to the arrival of the gulls, Erling and his colleagues recorded 171 species of land invertebrates (insects and spiders) on the island. A decade later, there were 354. As Erling wrote in one of his research reports, "Most invertebrate species were found in the gull colony and when compared with the sandy surfaces, the species composition is much more diverse."

This larger insect population, in turn, has made Surtsey a more suitable place for other birds to nest. Snow

buntings, for example, do not eat seafood as gulls do. They eat seeds and feed their young with insects. Early on, it was impossible for snow buntings to survive on Surtsey, for there were too few seeds and insects for them to utilize. Now that the gull colony is teeming with plant and insect life, however, snow buntings can survive here. They were first found nesting on Surtsey in 1996. Several other insectivore bird species are known to nest here now, too, including meadow pipits and white wagtails.

The gulls changed the soil, which increased its suitability for plants, which thrived and provided habitat for new and larger insect populations, which further enriched the soil. More plants moved in, and more insects moved in, and eventually, more bird species moved in, too. This process of change is called *succession,* and it has been monitored more closely on Surtsey than perhaps anywhere else in the world.

Once the first fifteen pitfall traps are set, Erling and Matthías return to the research hut. The other scientists are all out starting their own work, so the place is empty. The two have something to eat and something warm to drink, and they replenish their trap supplies. Then they head back out, this time to set pitfall traps on the north side of the island. It's late in the day now, and still raining. But

Fish bones (top) are a common sight in the bird colony, as are the empty (middle) and not-so-empty (bottom) nests of various gull species.

Among the seed-eating bird species now nesting on Surtsey are the snow bunting (*Plectrophenax nivalis*) above and the meadow pipit (*Anthus pratensis*) below. Both use insects to feed their young.

since the July sun doesn't set until eleven p.m. in Iceland, they've got plenty of time.

As they work, the scientists pass a surprising number of weather-beaten wooden stakes. The stakes tilt one way or the other, haphazardly marking . . . nothing. Or so it seems. In truth, the placement of these stakes is far from random. One hundred and twenty of them, of course, mark the corners of the thirty 10m-by-10m squares that Erling and Matthías have been setting pitfall traps in today. But dozens more mark places where new-to-the-island plants were recorded for the first time. On these stakes are notations, in permanent marker, recording the plant in question and the date of its discovery. In a way that only someone intimately familiar with Surtsey and its history could, Erling knows the purpose and history of almost every stake he passes. Every time he passes a stake marking a once-new arrival, he stops to assess the situation. Botanists will take an official record of this stake and the plant it marks later in the week, but Erling can't help but see for himself if the new plant has survived an Icelandic winter. Sometimes they have, and sometimes they haven't.

Eventually Erling and Matthias set the last pitfall trap. There are advantages, however, to being the last team to return to the hut. The portable heater is running, and the cabin is now warm and cozy. Borgþór has made porridge, and the table is set for eating. As each scientist spoons out a bowl, jazzes it up with raisins and cinnamon and milk, the stories start. Everyone shares what they've seen, what is new, and what has stayed the same—so far—on Surtsey.

After dinner, dishes are washed in rainwater that was collected from the roof and boiled just for the purpose. Leftovers are carried out to the refrigerator in the sand hole beside the hut. The table fills up again, but this time with notebooks for recording the day's observations and equipment being organized for the next day's work. Someone switches on a portable generator so that everyone can charge his or her computer and cell phone. The scientists rest, read, and talk. By ten o'clock it's still light outside, but everyone has slipped into his or her sleeping bunk. At some point the sun will set and this day will end . . . but the entire Surtsey team will be asleep by then.

A peek at the bunks in the research hut, taken before the team retired for the night.

The 2015 Surtsey Team

Icelandic custom dictates that all people be addressed by their first names only. Even though many of these scientists on the 2015 expedition team hold degrees that entitle them to be addressed as Doctor, the title is rarely used. In keeping with this tradition, the scientists you'll meet in this book are referred to only by their first name, and you'll find help for pronouncing those names on the right. To learn more about naming practices in Iceland—they're fascinating!—check out page 66.

As pictured on facing page, left to right

Erling Ólafsson
(ER-ling)
Entomologist

_____

Matthías Svavar Alfreðsson
(MA-tee-us)
Entomologist-in-training

_____

Loree Griffin Burns
(LOR-ee)
Children's book author

_____

Bjarni D. Sigurðsson
(BYAR-nee)
Soil chemist

_____

Kristján Jónasson
(KRIST-yown)
Geologist

_____

Sigurður H. Magnússon
(SEE-gur-thur)
Botanist

Lovísa Ásbjörnsdóttir
(LOW-vee-sa)
Geologist

_____

Þórdís Vilhelmina
Bragadóttir
(THOR-dis)
*Icelandic Environment
Agency representative*

_____

Paweł Wąsowicz
(PA-vou)
Botanist

_____

Borgþór Magnússon
(BORG-thor)
*Botanist and 2015
Surtsey mission head*

The boulder-strewn coastline, shown at the bottom of this image, is the place for going "more than pee." The research hut is located just out of the frame of this photo, to the left, and the peninsula (or spit) is located just out of the frame, to the right.

survival

By now you might be wondering about bathrooms on Surtsey. The bad news is that there aren't any, at least not the sort you're used to. The good news is that using the loo is like everything else on Surtsey: dramatic.

Behind the research hut, a small hole has been dug in the sand. (Don't worry, it's far from the food-cooling hole.) This is the men's urinal. And off the side porch, behind a wall of tall lava rocks, a similar hole marks the women's toilet.

The dining table in the hut doubles as a desk for working scientists.

These holes are for pee only, and no toilet paper is allowed. You can use toilet paper, of course—there's a roll on the kitchen counter in the hut—but it must be disposed of in the trash can inside the hut. The reason is probably obvious: scientists are here to observe and monitor a volcanic rock as it turns slowly into what we think of as earth. It's important that they not interfere with the very processes they are monitoring, or, at least, that they interfere as little as possible. Human urine changes the sand, in much the same way that bird excrement does. By being careful about where this urine is deposited, the scientists minimize their impact.

But what about number two? Anything more than pee requires a walk to the spit, the only Surtsey coast not separated from the ocean by tall lava cliffs. Instead, this low beach is edged with boulders that were rounded out and thrown ashore during and after the eruption that created the island. The rocky shoreline just before the peninsula begins is one of the most breathtaking places on Surtsey (see photo on page 34) . . . and it's also the place for going "more than pee."

North of Austurbunki lies the spit plain, a low peninsula surrounded by boulders that were worn smooth during Surtsey's eruption and which are constantly moved around by the sea.

The instructions for using these facilities are unsettling for a first-time visitor. Venture out onto the rocks—carefully, because they can shift—and find one small enough to lift. Lift it. Do your business into the hole beneath it; you can drop your used toilet paper in there, too. (Assuming you remembered to bring it with you from the hut!) Bury everything with the rock you lifted earlier. The perfect location will have you close enough to the ocean that the waves can come up and carry away your deposit at high tide, but not so close that the waves come while you're squatting there and carry *you* away. On a sunny summer day when the tide is low, "more than pee" is an adventure. On a rainy day with a raging sea, it's just not possible.

Tuesday, the second day of the 2015 expedition, dawns just that way: rainy, with a raging sea. Erling and Borgþór crawl out of their sleeping bags at seven a.m. to fire up the portable heater and start making breakfast. As the smell of frying bacon and toasting bread fills the hut, the others wake. The table is loaded with eggs, bacon, toast, yogurt, granola, juice, coffee, and, eventually, scientists. It's a quick meal, though, because everyone is eager to

get to work, despite the stormy weather. By 8:30 a.m., only Erling and Matthías are left in the hut.

"Rain is the enemy," Erling explains from his seat at the table.

His voice is quiet and matter-of-fact, without a trace of frustration. Day two is when Erling likes to begin sampling Surtsey's flying insects. Unfortunately, that's impossible in the rain. Flying insects don't fly when it's raining, and even if they did, wet nets are no good at catching them. So Erling and Matthías linger in the hut, preparing supplies they'll need later in the week and giving the sun a chance to come up and dry things out.

It doesn't.

So they adjust their plan. Erling decides they'll spend the morning handpicking—that is, collecting insects individually by hand. Teacher and student fill their pockets with glass vials of alcohol, tiny paintbrushes, and tweezers. Then they dress in rain gear and head for the spit.

The spit is the lowest point on Surtsey. Twice a day, high tides breach the walls around its edge and dump debris on its sandy middle. (Occasionally—especially during the winter months—stormy seas swamp the entire peninsula.) This regular interaction with the ocean is the main force driving life—and death—on this part of

The spit, as viewed from the top of Austurbunki.

Sea rocket (*Cakile arctica*) was the first plant found growing on Surtsey.

Lyme grass (*Leymus arenarius*) was the second species of plant to root in Surtsey's lava sand.

the island. Unlike the gull colony, where organisms arrive mainly by air, here on the spit, organisms arrive mostly by sea. They float in on the waves or raft in on objects floating on those waves.

Much like excrement and food scraps in the gull colony, the seaweed and marine organisms that the waves dump on the spit decompose and add nutrients to the sand here. Any seeds that arrive will land in soil that's a little richer than it is farther inland. When those seeds germinate, the plants they produce mark a tiny first step toward the building up of a living community on the spit. The first seeds found on Surtsey were collected at the high-tide line on the spit in 1964, just months after Surtsey formed. Scientists didn't stay long on the island back then, because its volcanoes were still erupting violently. But they collected these seeds and planted them in pots back on the mainland . . . and were delighted when the seeds produced plants.

Would more seeds eventually arrive on the spit?

Would any of these *germinate* on the spit?

The very next year, a living plant was found growing on the spit. But the tiny pioneering seedling, called a sea rocket, was soon suffocated by falling ash from the still-erupting volcanoes. In 1966 a second sea rocket plant was found on the spit, as well as the plant of a new species—lyme grass. Both plants grew just at the high-tide line, suggesting that the seeds they came from had floated to Surtsey on ocean waves. The same sea that brought life to the spit, however, took it away again. "The colonizers were wiped out by ocean waves sweeping over the low and sandy beach," wrote Sturla Friðriksson, the botanist who had found both plants.

But each year brought new seeds, and soon several species of plants grew on the spit. Sometimes these plants lived to maturity. Sometimes they produced flowers, and even seeds. Occasionally they were able to spread their seeds—and thus their kind—farther in on the island. When winters were easy and storms were few, a simple community evolved on the spit. But that community was—and still is—completely

Things on the spit can change drastically from year to year. For two examples, compare plant life there in 2009 (top left) with plant life in 2013 (top right), or the overall shape of the spit in 2014 (bottom left) with its shape in 2015 (bottom right).

at the mercy of the ocean. Waves regularly change the size and shape of the spit, they regularly deposit new life on the island, and they regularly destroy that very same life. The ocean gives, and the ocean takes away. The spit is the place on Surtsey where this is most obvious.

Insects and spiders are regularly found on the spit, too. They arrive much like seeds and plants do, floating in on air currents or waves, hitching a ride on a bird, or rafting on debris. Once here, they face the same harsh conditions that plants do. They thrive while they can. Some, like aphids, are often found in the mounds of plants that spring up each year. Others rely on microenvironments that are unique to the debris-strewn spit, such as the moist underside of decaying planks and boards that have washed ashore. Today, Erling and Matthías plan to find and sample these creatures.

"The spit is pretty stable," Erling says as he surveys the low beach. "Usually there is not much new to find here. The new stuff usually happens in the gull colony."

But that won't stop him from looking. Through the gray drizzle, he watches Matthías head down the beach toward the tip of the peninsula, and then he turns his attention to the part of the spit he'll be surveying. He spots a wooden plank that looks promising: it's buried in the sand a bit, but not so deep as to be difficult to move. He pulls his tools from his pocket as he approaches the board, then drops to his knees beside it.

Erling collects insects on the spit one at a time, and by hand (left). Among the insects he finds are tiny springtails (above), only a millimeter or two in length, which thrive on the wet underside of beached driftwood.

Paintbrush in hand, he flips the board and leans in to study its sandy underside. After a few seconds he sees the movement he is looking for: tiny, delicate invertebrates called springtails. He opens his collection vial, dips the tip of the brush into the alcohol inside, then gently touches the wet bristles to a springtail body. The tiny springtail sticks to the wet brush, allowing Erling to easily lift it from the board and deposit it in his collection vial. He takes several more springtails this way, then replaces the board exactly as he found it.

Erling scours several more planks, then scans piles of trash and mounds of green sandwort plants with equal vigor. He collects a few more springtails and some aphids too. He also finds sturdier invertebrates—tiny beetles and bright red spider mites—and gently collects them with tweezers. These are all creatures that are unlikely to fall into the pitfall traps he set yesterday, so handpicking is the only way to sample them.

Erling thinks of the insects he finds here year after year as old friends. He doesn't think he's found any new species today, but knowing for sure will require patient examination of the entire collection under a microscope. This is work he'll do later, back in his lab on the mainland. He collects so many insects on each Surtsey trip that there is currently a large backlog; Erling is still identifying species collected in the summer of 2007! This is just one of the reasons he's so grateful to have a capable student like Matthías working with him.

The bright coloring of this tiny spider mite makes it fairly easy to spot against the gray rocks and dark sand of the spit.

Matthías is twenty-nine years old and has been studying entomology with Erling for two years. Last year, as a beginning student in Erling's lab, he was invited to Surtsey for the first time. He knew the moment he arrived that it would not be his last summer here. In fact, at the end of the weeklong 2014 expedition, Matthías intentionally left his pillow and sleeping bag behind in the research hut.

"Why did I do that? I think it was a clear message: I was going to return to Surtsey," he says. "I don't plan to ever bring them home!"

Matthías is a quiet scientist, observant and patient. He watches Erling carefully, always eager to emulate his mentor's technique and soak up Erling's knowledge.

"I have learned more from him in the past year than in all my courses so far," Matthías says.

Matthías walking on the spit.

It's clear that the mentor admires the student just as much.

"Matti has an intensity of interest," Erling says. "A curiosity. And he doesn't watch the clock."

This means a lot to Erling. Surveying insects in the field for five days is not an easy job. It requires great patience and intense focus. It requires working in the rain, in the sun, in the cold and the heat, in the daytime, and sometimes into the night. Occasionally it allows for proper dinner breaks; often it doesn't. The work requires passion and dedication, and Matthías is a natural. As an added bonus, he has sharp eyes.

"Matti sees more than I do," Erling admits with a smile. "He has younger eyes."

When Erling and Matthías meet up in the middle of the spit, each having surveyed his assigned area, they talk in quiet tones about what they've turned up. A lot of the usual suspects, they think. They murmur about springtails and mites and roundworms as they head back to the research hut.

Iceland requires all citizens to retire from their jobs on their seventieth birthday. For Erling, that's just a few years away. He doesn't actually plan to stop his work on Surtsey—he expects to join future expeditions as a photographer, continuing the pictorial history he's amassed over the past forty-five years.

"I'm certainly not going to start golfing when I retire!" he jokes. "I'll keep on coming to Surtsey."

A disturbing amount of trash washes ashore on Surtsey every year.

But he does recognize that it's time to train his replacement, someone who will continue to survey the insects on Surtsey in the decades to come.

On their way back to the hut, even though their collecting is done for the day, Erling occasionally stops in the middle of a sentence, grabs for his tweezers, and drops to his knees. He stabs at the sand, usually coming up with an insect even Matthías hadn't seen.

"You can develop this ability to see. You just have to know what to look for," he says, "and where to look."

After a long day of collecting

insects on the spit in the rain and an even longer trip to the gull colony to set up another type of insect trap, Erling and Matthías finally return to the hut. Matthías unpacks the day's samples, labeling and preparing them for transport back to the lab. Erling starts frying fish enough for the entire team to eat for dinner. A lovely aroma has begun to fill the hut when two unexpected things happen: the sun comes out, and Þórdís brings a message from the spit.

"Come quick," Þórdís tells Erling. "Borgþór says to bring your camera."

It can only mean one thing: a new species.

Since Erling recorded the first birds bred on Surtsey—the black guillemot chicks he discovered in 1970—fifteen species of birds have been found breeding here. Scientists suspect that other species might be breeding on the island, but definitive proof has yet to be found. For example, Erling had earlier found a cracked eggshell in the gull colony, and it looked like an eider duck egg. Were eider ducks nesting on Surtsey or did a gull steal an eider duck egg from a nest on a nearby island and fly it over to Surtsey to eat? Intriguingly, scientists later found the dead carcass of an adult male eider duck on the island. Had he been breeding on Surtsey? It was impossible to know for sure. In order to add eider duck to the list of Surtsey's breeding birds, scientists would need to find an actual eider duck nest. Better still, they'd need to find eider duck eggs or chicks.

It turns out that an eider duck chick is exactly what Borgþór has spotted! Three eider duck chicks, in fact, waddling along behind their mother on the spit. Erling arrives in time to verify the find, and he captures the little family on film.

"This was the perfect plan," Erling jokes on the way back to the cabin, his trusty camera still around his neck. He'd helped the team collect definitive proof that eider ducks were breeding on Surtsey. "And when we get back to the hut, someone else will have finished cooking the dinner!"

Erling (foreground, with camera) and Borgþór scan the coast for a family of eider ducks. They eventually collect proof that eider ducks are breeding on Surtsey (facing page).

The view of Austurbunki from its base. The lighthouse can be seen to the left of the main peak.

change

I n the wee hours of Wednesday morning, the sun rises over Surtsey for the first time all week. After two days of raw and rainy data collection, Erling and Matthías are thrilled. Finally they can use their nets and begin sampling the island's flying insects. The grassiest site they'll sample— the gull colony—needs time to dry out, so they head first to the base of Austurbunki. They'll begin the day's collecting at its peak, in the second of the three man-made structures on Surtsey: the lighthouse.

Erling at work.

Textures on the surface of Austurbunki.

Steaming fissures are a common sight on a hike of Austurbunki.

When Surtsey burst out of the ocean unannounced in 1963, people who lived and sailed in the area worried that the island, not drawn on any existing nautical maps, could cause a disastrous accident. After years of debate, a lighthouse was erected on top of Austurbunki. But something was wrong with the hood—the part of the structure that held the light—and it exploded during its very first year of service. It was repaired, but something was still not right, and it exploded again. Enthusiasm for the lighthouse waned, and it was not repaired a second time. Forty years later, its cement foundation still sits on top of Austurbunki. Erling thinks it's an eyesore and sincerely hopes it will be removed one day. For now, though, he's not above putting it to good use, but to do so, he and Matthías have to climb up to it.

The sides of Austurbunki are steep but remarkably stable. This is no longer the mountain of delicate tephra that piled up back in 1963. Thanks to the volcano's searing heat, the tephra that didn't blow or wash away was turned into a tougher substance that scientists call *palagonite tuff*. It's basically a very hard and very dense rock.

Erling and Matthías hike up Austurbunki's five hundred feet (155 meters) of palagonite tuff with ease. Steam rises from small cracks under their feet, and strange textures abound. The palagonite is a difficult surface for plants to grow on—the few that spring up in its sandy cracks don't survive long—so there is not much insect habitat here. As a result, there is little insect sampling to do along the way. The top of Austurbunki is a slightly different story.

The view from the top is stunning, particularly on a sunny and clear morning like this one. Surtsey's neighbor islands rise from a sparkling ocean, and beyond them one can see the outlines of Iceland's mainland volcanoes. The view of

Surtsey itself is spectacular from this vantage, too. The spit, the craters, the gull colony, *Vesturbunki*—even the research hut—are breathtaking from above. If you're a scientist doing field research, this might just be the most spectacular "field" of them all.

The lighthouse foundation is an empty cement square with two openings: a large door and a small window. When Erling and Matthías reach it, they step inside and carefully scrutinize every corner for insects.

"The lighthouse is an excellent trap for just-arrived flying insects," Erling explains.

Although it's possible for flying insects to make it to Surtsey under their own power, especially from nearby islands, a more likely scenario is for them to arrive on the wind. Strong winds can blow in insects that might not make it to Surtsey otherwise. If this kind of strong wind event happens in a given year, Erling gets a

The view to the north from the top of Austurbunki includes the Icelandic mainland, several other islands, and the sparkling blue North Atlantic.

Erling and Matthías look for insects both inside and outside the lighthouse.

preview of it here in the lighthouse. Ten years ago, in 2005, a large number of insect species not previously found on Surtsey were found in the gull colony. It's unusual for so many new species to arrive at once, and scientists were intrigued. When Erling and his collegues discovered many individuals of these same new species in the lighthouse, they knew a wind event had blown them in. Wind events such as these don't happen every year, but if they do, and if the wind carried insects onto the island, Erling will find out when he explores the lighthouse.

"It's extremely useful to know when winds bring a new shipment of insects to Surtsey," Erling says.

This year, they find no insects inside the lighthouse. Erling and Matthías go back and examine the outside area, sweeping their nets through what little vegetation there is. When Austurbunki has been sampled to their satisfaction, the two scientists head to their next destination: the craters of Surtur and Surtungur.

"Do you know the song 'It's Oh So Quiet' by Björk?" Erling asks when they reach the lip of Surtungur. "This place reminds me of it. It's one of my favorite spots on the island."

Sure enough, as soon as Erling and Matthías descend into the crater, it becomes oh, so quiet. The raucous sounds of the bird colony and of the Atlantic Ocean smashing against lava cliffs—soundtracks to life on Surtsey—disappear, as if the scientists had dropped into a soundproof room. The deeper they climb, the louder the silence gets. A few fulmars nesting in the top walls of the crater start to complain when they notice the intruding entomologists, but the only other sound is of hiking boots on lava, with the occasional swish of a sweep net.

As they'd done on the spit the day before, Erling and Matthías part without speaking, each confidently sampling a different part of the crater. They work separately, but with an identical technique: spot an insect,

The view from Austurbunki, looking to the south. Just before the lush green of the gull colony sits the crater of the Surtur volcano.

Erling collecting insect samples inside the Surtungur crater.

freeze, lift the net, slip into a crouch. When the moment is right, the wrist flicks, a free hand closes off the net and secures the handle against the ground, and the other hand slips into a pocket in search of a collection vial.

Erling points out familiar landmarks as he works in the crater—the site of the first raven nest ever found on Surtsey, the site of a more recent raven nest, and a small fissure he calls the Oven. Forty-five years ago, during his first summer on Surtsey, Erling and his colleagues were able to put a hot dog on a pole and slide it into the Oven, using its intense heat to barbecue their dinner. To show how much has changed here in all those years, Erling climbs into the Oven to pose for a picture.

The next stop is the gull colony. Erling and Matthías collect insects along the way, stopping now and then to transfer into collection vials the flies and, less frequently, wasps and moths they've caught. The vegetation grows denser as they reach the edge of the colony, of course, and the number of insects on the wing picks up, too. Time crawls as the scientists do their work. Gulls swoop and screech overhead. The ocean crashes against the lava cliffs. The sun shines on all of it. Somewhere to the south of this place,

A closer view of Surtungur. This photo was taken from the edge of the crater.

the rest of the world is bustling. Here, time slows as Erling and Matthías methodically collect insects in the lush green grass.

Near the far end of the gull colony, Matthías spots a rusted rectangle of corrugated tin lying flat on the grass. Erling guesses that it blew in from its storage spot under the research hut, probably during a winter storm. The two men can barely contain their excitement over this seemingly uninteresting development. They drop their nets and their backpacks, kneel together in the tall grass, one on either side of the sheet of tin. Then, a quick countdown in Icelandic . . .

"Þrír, tveir, einn—"

. . . and they flip the sheet, tossing it aside and leaning in to grab what they can. Startled insects hop and flit

After this gull died of natural causes, its carcass became a temporary home for a variety of insects. Erling and Matthías couldn't help but check them out . . . and collect a few samples.

and flicker in the newly exposed grass, and Erling and Matthías tackle them as quickly—and as gently—as possible. The flurry of captures is funny to watch, especially when Erling slips a filled vial into his pocket and declares, hands over his head in a victory salute, "We won!"

Not long after, the pair stumbles upon another exciting find: a gull carcass. Dead bodies can be a bonanza for entomologists because the carcasses are quickly colonized by scavenger insects. Any plans for a lunch break are forgotten as the two scientists' entomology instincts take over. They flip the gull carcass, shake out several flies and a small pile of blowfly larvae, then bottle each and every one.

Erling and Matthías do eventually eat lunch, but soon after, they are back in the gull colony. It's the center of insect life and so the center of their collecting. They've already set pitfall traps here, and a tent trap, and earlier this morning they'd collected flying insects with their nets. What could possibly be left for them to do? Handpicking, just as they did on the spit yesterday.

There are several species of insects known to live in the gull colony that can only be collected individually. Weevils, for example, don't fly, so they won't turn up in a sweep net. And since they spend their entire lives crawling on a single plant, they're unlikely to end up in a pitfall trap either. In order to collect these critters, Erling has to pick them up one by one. He starts by finding a mound of scurvy grass and settling down next to it. Then he unpacks a couple of special collecting tools, along with his glasses, and peers closely at the plant. He finds signs of weevils right away: weevil larvae chew tunnels in scurvy leaves, and these tunnels turn brown and are easy to see. It's not long, though, before he spots adult weevils too.

This particular species of weevil is too small and delicate to collect with tweezers but too big for the paintbrush technique Erling used to collect springtails earlier in the week. How, then, to collect them? Simple: he sticks a suction tool in his mouth and sucks them up one by one. Don't worry. There's a barrier inside the flexible straw–like tube of his suction tool, so there's no chance he'll swallow a weevil. He simply sucks each weevil gently up into the tube, then blows it gently out into his collection vial.

Meanwhile, Matthías unfurls a flag of white fabric, lays it on the grass, and drags it around behind him. The flag is called a tick sheet, and it's great for collecting tiny invertebrates that live in the long grass and are otherwise difficult to capture. He drags the sheet for what feels like a very long time, collecting, for this effort, a single mite. It's much too small to identify on-site, so he adds it to the growing collection of 2015 insect samples to be examined back in the lab.

Erling and Matthías spend almost every waking moment of their third day on the island collecting insects. They capture hundreds. The most exciting, by far, are several moths of the species *Cochylis dubitana*. This species has never been collected on Surtsey before. Nor has the moth species *Scrobipalpa samadensis*, which Matthías finds in the early evening in the lava sand close to the hut. Later, over a dinner of pasta and meat sauce, the entire expedition team toasts the two new insect species. Another day on Surtsey comes to a close.

Collecting weevils (left).

An adult weevil on a scurvy grass leaf (below). The light yellow tracks were left by larval weevils that once fed on the leaf.

Erling, surrounded by wooden marking stakes, collects a pitfall trap from the lava sand on Surtsey.

departure

The last full on-island workday feels special from the beginning. The sun has returned, accounting for some of the brightness. But there are other signs, too. The door of the research hut is opened wide during breakfast, and through it drifts the happy, husky warbling of a snow bunting. Later, Borgþór retrieves a shovel from under the hut and starts to dig in the sand near the "fridge," eventually unearthing—or, rather, "un-lavasanding"—a large plastic bag.

Matthías at work.

On the last full working day on Surtsey, Erling and Matthías collect the pitfall traps they set earlier in the week. The task takes Erling through a variety of landscapes on the north side of the island, including plots in thick lava sand (top left), the wet lava sand on the spit (top right), a field of sharp lava formations (this type of hardened lava is called a'a lava; bottom left), and the weedy area surrounding the helicopter landing pad (bottom right).

"Dinner," he says mysteriously, carrying it into the hut.

Back inside, Matthías takes his time packing up for one final day in the field. He and Erling have decided to separate for the morning, each retrieving half of the pitfall traps they set on the first day of the expedition. Matthías will collect traps on the south side of the island, and he sets out first. As he walks away from the hut alone, Erling smiles like a father watching his kid go off to kindergarten.

"You always see insects when you forget your net," he says, pointing to the one Matthías left propped on the porch.

Erling will collect traps on the north side of the island. He begins in a lyme grass habitat very close to the hut. His procedure is pretty much the reverse of the one he used to set the traps four days earlier: he photographs the plot from its edge, marches in, kneels next to the trap, disassembles the tented lid, and lifts out the plastic cup. Because he can't help himself, he peeks inside each cup briefly, hoping to see a new insect or two. Eventually he drops a handwritten label—plot number and date—into each cup. Then he adds a splash of alcohol, snaps a lid onto the container, and drops it into his backpack. He'll examine each and every insect more closely back in his laboratory.

As he works, Erling shares a few theories that might explain why a moth that is fairly common in Iceland—*Cochylis dubitana*—was found on Surtsey only this year. He and Matthías netted several specimens in the gull colony yesterday. Why have they never seen this common moth here before?

The first two theories are quite simple. Although scientific expeditions have come to Surtsey every year since 1965, there have been many years when no insects were sampled. Between 1972 and 1984, for example, Erling visited the island only three times. If the *Cochylis dubitana* moth lived here during those years, it would have been easy to miss it. Second, it's possible that it simply took

A pitfall trap just before Erling collects it from the lava sand (top). The trap itself is a plastic jar, which in this image can be seen buried in the lava sand under the plastic disc labeled R16. Erling pulls the trap jar from the sand, adds a label, and secures everything with a lid (bottom). All the insects that fell into the trap during the week are now safely preserved and easy to transport back to Erling's lab on the mainland.

An adult *Cochylis dubitana* moth. This image was not collected on Surtsey but elsewhere in Iceland. Notice the moth rests with its wings folded over its body. In the schematic below, which shows all the stages of the *C. dubitana* life cycle, the adult moth is shown with its wings open, as in flight.

Larva

Egg

Life Cycle
of a
Cochylis dubitana Moth

Pupa

this species an extraordinarily long time to make its way to the island. The third theory is the one weighing most heavily on Erling's mind today. He shares it out loud during his last morning of fieldwork.

"You never know what you are missing—" he starts. He explains that he and Matthías monitor insects on Surtsey for just five days every July. So, for the remaining 360 days of the year no one is monitoring insect life here. Who knows what flies or crawls along the island on those days? No one. But sometimes conditions on Surtsey change unexpectedly, just enough to allow resident but undetected insects to be noticed.

This year, for example, was a strange one in Iceland. The entire country, including Surtsey, experienced a late spring. Unusually cold temperatures lingered well into the month of June, delaying the growth and development of both plants and insects, including such moths as *Cochylis dubitana*.

Moths have a four-part life cycle: egg, larva (caterpillar), pupa, adult. This life cycle in *C. dubitana* is perfectly timed with the seasons. The insects spend the winter in the pupal stage. Early in spring, the adult moths emerge and begin to fly. In a typical Icelandic summer this would happen in early June. The adult moths live for only a couple of weeks, just enough time to mate and produce a new generation of eggs. These eggs hatch caterpillars during the month of July, and the caterpillars spend the rest of the summer eating and growing on their host plants. Come fall, the fully grown caterpillars form pupae and the cycle begins anew.

As you know, Erling and Matthías always visit Surtsey for a single week in early July. It makes sense that in most years, they'd never see *C. dubitana* moths, even if the moths were living on the island; in a typical year, the adults are in the flying stage of their life cycle only in June. According to Erling's new theory, however,

this year's late spring may have delayed the entire *C. dubitana* life cycle. Adult moths that would normally have emerged earlier in the spring emerged instead at the end of June . . . and a few of those adult moths were still alive in early July, when the 2015 expedition team arrived.

The way to avoid missing insects in this way, at least in Erling's mind, is to visit Surtsey more frequently. It might be hard for him to stay for the entire summer, as he did when he was in his twenties, but he could easily make three trips a season: one in June, one in July, and one in August. He's convinced that if he did, he would collect a lot of insects so far undocumented on Surtsey.

In support of this theory, Erling tells a couple of stories. In 2011 he accompanied a documentary film-making crew to Surtsey in the month of June. As the crew collected the footage they needed for their film, Erling collected insects. (It's just what entomologists do!) He found specimens of two fly species that had never before been seen on Surtsey. Two years later, he had the chance to go in September, with a German tele-

Surtsey's Lava

Lavas are classified by their mineral composition, and Surtsey's lava is high in silica, iron, and magnesium; it's called basaltic lava. Basaltic lava is further divided into three types, two of which are visible on the island. A'a (pronounced AH-ah) lava is very thick and, as a result, slow-moving. When it cools, it hardens into sharp, pointed peaks that can be treacherous to navigate on foot. (See page 58.) Pahoehoe (pronounced pa-HOY-HOY) lava is markedly less viscous than a'a lava and so flows faster. When it hardens, the rock it forms has a smooth surface that is sometimes described as "ropy." The third type of basaltic lava, called pillow lava, forms when lava flows under the sea.

vision crew. That time he found a new-to-Surtsey spider.

"You never know what you are missing," Erling repeats. "I need to make three expeditions every summer."

He collects one pitfall trap sample after another, dreaming all the while of longer and more frequent visits, allowing him to do more sampling and, therefore, have a fuller picture of the insects that call the island home, the habitats they live in, and the ecosystems they are helping to create.

The final two traps that Erling collects are back up near the research hut, in a bed of very sharp and hard-to-navigate lava known as a'a lava. The formations here are speckled with mosses and lichens that are pretty enough to take Erling's attention away from his insects; he pauses between traps to take a few photos.

Shortly after, Matthías and Erling regroup at the hut, catch up on the morning's collections, and pack away their samples. By the time they are ready to head back outside, clouds have blotted out the sun and a cold wind has picked up. They add a few layers of clothes and join Borgþór, Þórdís, and Bjarni for their very last data collection task of the 2015 expedition: the annual nest count.

Before the expedition leaves, Bjarni does some routine repairs on the weather tower.

The small team heads for the gull colony, Borgþór carrying a tall walking stick, a tape measure, and a clipboard. They pass the a'a lava bed and Surtsey's weather tower (the third man-made structure on the island) and head to the outer edges of the gull colony, where Surtsey's resident lesser black-backed gulls and herring gulls nest.

To begin the count, Borgþór plants his stick in the very center of the plot, then hooks the end of his tape measure over a nail at its top end. While he secures the end this way, Bjarni takes the other end of the tape measure out to a distance of 58.5 feet (17.85 meters). The other three nest hunters line up between Bjarni and Borgþór, along the length of the tape measure, and face the same direction. On Borgþór's signal, they begin to walk in a circle, scanning the ground in front of their feet for gull nests and shouting out when they've found one. They make a complete circle; Borgþór records their findings. They repeat this procedure in each plot within the gull colony until they've counted nests in all of them. They find dozens of nests, and even a few chicks, hiding in the rocks.

Ever on the lookout for new life here, Bjarni—a soil scientist with a passion for fungi—spots a flush of mushrooms hidden in the long grass. The nest counters take a break as Bjarni records the find.

Bjarni, Erling, Matthías, and Þórdís survey bird nests in the gull colony (top left) while Borgþór anchors their measuring tape and tallies their results (top right). The team stumbles on a gull chick hiding in its nest.

By the time the nest count is done, the sky is spitting a cold rain. Matthías and Erling decide to pull down the tent trap they set up earlier in the week now, instead of waiting until morning. (It's much easier to work with when it's dry.) Eventually the whole team trudges back to the hut, loaded down with the tent trap, insect samples, and nesting information.

Bjarni and Matthías stop to get a closer look at mushrooms found hidden in the thick grass of the gull colony. The mushroom *Galerina pseudomycenopsis* (called *dýjakveif* in Icelandic) had not been found on Surtsey before this discovery.

Inside, the heater is running again and the entire expedition team assembles. They've each completed their on-island work for the year, and it's officially time to celebrate. There is a ceremonial cleaning of the dining table (no errant fly wings allowed!), and Borgþór carves the precooked leg of lamb that he'd lifted out of the sand earlier in the day. Someone lights a candle; someone else folds fancy paper napkins and sets them beside plastic wineglasses on the table. Soon the table is set with boiled red potatoes, gravy, beans, cabbage, salad, and rhubarb jam, too. Before the scientists take their seats, Borgþór offers a toast to their successful mission.

"*Skál!*" the team shouts in unison, lifting their glasses to cheer a job well done. (You guessed it: *Skál!* means "Cheers!" in Icelandic.)

Tonight's is the longest dinner of the week, with conversation in both Icelandic and English, and lots of laughter. A toast is made to each new plant discovered (*Alchemilla alpina* and *Carex bigelowii*), and to each new insect (*Cochylis dubitana* and *Scrobipalpa samadensis*), and, of course, to the eider duck (*Somateria mollissima*). A toast is made to Surtsey itself, too. As the candle burns low, the scientists laugh and joke and talk their way through their farewell night.

In the morning, the 2015 expedition team will pack up everything they've brought here, as well as the samples and data they've collected. They'll clean up the hut, close its shutters again, lock its door. They'll cart their equipment and supplies down to the shore, past the lyme grass and the a'a lava and the more-than-pee beach. On the spit, they'll take turns lugging their gear to the rock wall and over it. They'll collect bright orange buoys that have washed up as debris on the spit (the Icelandic Coast Guard can reuse them). They'll snack on hard-boiled eggs and enjoy the curious seals that pop out of the ocean to stare at them. When the Coast Guard ship that will bring them back to the mainland finally glides into view, they'll stand and begin the journey back to older Earth, carrying with them a whole lot of information about life on this upstart island.

Appendices

Icelandic Names

As you've read, the bestowing of names is a special task for Icelandic parents. Moms and dads take their time choosing the perfect first name for their baby boys and baby girls. You might be surprised to learn that parents are not allowed to choose just any old name. Rather, they have to pick one from lists of approved Icelandic names. It's illegal to give a boy a name from the girls list, or vice versa, or to give any child a name that is not on the lists at all. Occasionally Icelandic parents decide to choose a new name anyway, but in order to do so legally, they must appeal to the Icelandic Personal Names Committee for approval. And in order for a new name to be considered, it must contain only letters found in the Icelandic alphabet, it mustn't be derogatory in any way, and it must work grammatically with the Icelandic language.

The bestowing of last names is unique in Iceland, too. These are not handed down from parent to child, as they are in America. Instead, they are built anew using the first name of one of the baby's parents. Erling's father was Ólafur, and so Erling was given the last name Ólafsson. It means son of Ólafur. Erling's brothers have this same last name. His two sisters, however, are not sons of Ólafur. They are the daughters of Ólafur, and so their last names are Ólafsdóttir.

Another thing you should know about names in Iceland: almost everyone goes by his or her first name alone. If the current president of Iceland, Guðni Thorlacius Jóhannesson, visited your school, for example, you might be tempted to address him very formally. (*Hello, President Jóhannesson!*) But this just isn't the custom in Iceland. Instead, everyone—bus drivers, doctors, teachers, janitors, professors, presidents, mothers, fathers, aunts, uncles, brothers, sisters, everyone—is called by his or her first name, all the time and in all situations. Even the phone book is organized by first names! So, if you're lucky enough to meet the president of Iceland one day, just shake his hand and say "Hello, Guðni!" Of course, you'd have to figure out how to pronounce that. So read on . . .

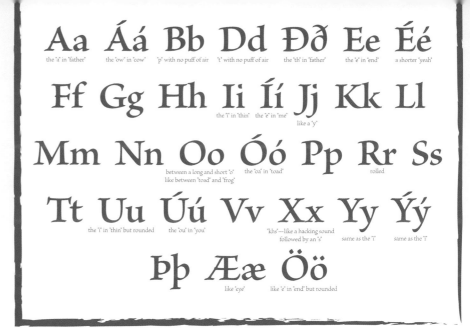

The Icelandic Alphabet

You may have noticed unusual letters and symbols in the Icelandic words used in this book. The name of the town where Erling grew up is a good example: Hafnarfjörður. These letters and symbols are part of the Icelandic alphabet.

There are thirty-two letters in all, and most of them are familiar. A few letters appear twice, once as we are used to seeing them and a second time in accented forms. Each form has its own pronunciation. For example, the unaccented letter *a* is pronounced "ah," as in the word *father*, but the accented letter *á* is pronounced "ow," as in the word *cow*.

A few of the letters in the Icelandic alphabet don't exist in our alphabet. These include ð (pronounced like the "th" sound in the English word *father*), þ (also pronounced like the "th," but more like in the English word *think*), and æ (pronounced like the English word *eye*). So when you meet the Icelandic president, Guðni Thorlacius Jóhannesson, you can now pronounce his name with confidence. Right?

One last thing: You may have noticed that several of the letters in our alphabet don't appear in the Icelandic one. These include *c, q, w,* and *z.* You may also have noticed that one of the scientists on Surtsey was named Paweł. What's up with that? Well, Paweł hails from Poland, and the Polish alphabet does, indeed, have a *w.* Yet I can't help but mention that a Polish *w* is pronounced like our English *v.* And that *ł*? That's pronounced like our English *w.* Aren't languages fascinating?

Across a Year and Around a Day

The schematic on page 2 shows the Earth at four different points on its 365-day orbit around the sun. As you can see, at a certain point during that trip, Iceland and the entire Northern Hemisphere are tilted away from the sun. At this time, these places experience what we call winter. Six months later, when Earth has moved to the opposite end of its orbit, the situation will be reversed: Iceland and the Northern Hemisphere are now tilted toward the sun. It is tempting to think, then, that the average temperature differences between winter and summer are tied to the Earth's distance from the sun. But, as I learned while writing this book, it's more complicated than that. At the point on the Earth's orbit that the Northern Hemisphere is tilted away from the sun and experiencing winter, the planet as a whole is actually three million

miles *closer* to the sun! Likewise, when the Northern Hemisphere is tilted toward the sun and experiencing summer, the planet is three million miles *farther* from the source of those rays.

What, then, causes seasonal differences on Earth?

The answer lies in the angle at which the sun's rays hit the planet. When the sun's rays hit the Earth straight on (that is, at a 90° angle), the land those rays strike experiences a certain amount of warming energy. As the angle at which the sun's rays strike the planet strays from 90°, however, this warming energy is spread over a much larger area. (You can visualize this by pointing a flashlight directly at a wall. When the light strikes the wall at a 90° angle, you'll see a compact circle of light. If you move your flashlight so that its light beam hits the wall at an angle, however, the circle of light stretches into an oval.) Spreading the same warming energy over a larger area means each location within that area experiences less of that energy. What's more, rays that strike the Earth at the largest angles deliver the least warming. (In the flashlight experiment, this would correspond to the uppermost edge of the oval.) And so the Northern Hemisphere experiences lower average temperatures during seasonal winter and higher average temperatures during seasonal summer.

As the Earth orbits the sun, it also spins on an imaginary axis. One full spin takes about twenty-four hours, and it is this turning that gives the planet its days and nights. While a land mass is facing the sun, it will experience what we call daytime. As the Earth spins, however, that same land will eventually face away from the sun and, as a result, experience what we call nighttime. Because of the way the planet is tilted, locations near its top (north pole) or bottom (south pole) will, at certain times of the year, spend an extended part of each twenty-four-hour day in daytime (for example, Iceland during the northern summer) or in nighttime (for example, Iceland during the northern winter).

Westman Islands

The Westman Islands are an archipelago of fifteen islands and more than thirty small rocky outcroppings (called skerries) and spires (called pinnacles) located off the southwest coast of Iceland, very near to Surtsey. The largest of these, and the only inhabited island in the archipelago, is Heimaey. Its name means "Home Island," and its surface is home to forty-five hundred Icelanders. They have their own school, airport, golf course, stores, hotels, and museums. A ferry to Heimaey from the mainland takes about thirty minutes.

Heimaey was formed thousands of years ago—in much the same way as Surtsey was—when the volcano now called Helgafell erupted out of the sea. Helgafell is a big part of the landscape of Heimaey, and it was assumed to be extinct. But in January 1973 an eruption began in the middle of the night. As with the eruption that formed Surtsey, there was no warning. The entire island of Heimaey had to be evacuated, homes were buried in lava, and the harbor itself was saved only by the relentless efforts of a few brave residents who stayed behind to pump gallons and gallons of seawater over the advancing lava. The cone of the new volcano, called Eldfell, now sits beside Helgafell, dominating the landscape of Heimaey.

One famous resident of Heimaey today is Toti, an Atlantic puffin living at the island's natural history museum. The Westman Islands are part of a handful of rocky Arctic islands on which Atlantic puffins nest, and millions of them return to Heimaey every summer to breed. In 2011, baby Toti, unable to migrate to wintering grounds on the open ocean with the rest of the puffins, was rescued by island residents, and he now lives at the museum, educating and entertaining the tourists who pass through Heimaey.

This photo was taken from the coast of Heimaey, looking south toward Surtsey. The visible islands include, from the left, Stórhöfði, Suðurey, Geirfuglasker, Surtsey, Brandur, and Álsey.

More Recent Upstarts

Prior to the eruption that formed Surtsey, and for about ten thousand years before that, the tiny top of the undersea volcano called Nishinoshima poked out of the Pacific Ocean. Located about 620 miles (1,000 kilometers) south of Tokyo, Japan, this dot of land, barely an island, was part of the Bonin Islands chain. In May 1973 a new vent opened up on Nishinoshima, and its eruption created a much bigger island. Japanese scientists studied the island, also named Nishinoshima, intermittently in the decades after this eruption. More recently, in November 2013, the volcano rumbled to life again. A new island emerged from the sea, was quickly named Niijima (Japanese for "new island"), and just as quickly merged with the existing island of Nishinoshima. As of November 2015 the eruption was still under way and the island was still growing.

Elsewhere in the Pacific, in the archipelago of islands that make up the Kingdom of Tonga, another upstart island is in the making. This mile-long island was first reported in January 2015, but by May, scientists in the area were already predicting its demise. The eruption that formed this island has yet to produce lava, so its delicate tephra will slowly wash away and blow back into the sea.

Research Update

In July 2019, forty-nine years after he first stepped onto her shores, Erling Ólafsson returned to Surtsey to survey invertebrates. He and Matthías Alfreðsson recorded two new species—a spider and a bumblebee—and other members of the expedition team recorded a new plant species. Two months later Erling celebrated his seventieth birthday. Even though he is officially retired, no one believes he is finished with Surtsey, least of all his protégé Matthías, who insists, "The island is too close to his heart."

Matthías and Erling on Surtsey in July of 2019.

Glossary

a'a lava (pronounced: AH-ah). When molten lava cools and hardens, it can take on a variety of shapes, textures, and colors, depending on its composition and on environmental conditions; a'a lava hardens in razor-sharp peaks and projections that are very difficult to walk over. The a'a lava on Surtsey ripped up the author's favorite hiking shoes!

alcohol. A liquid that can be used to preserve insects.

archipelago. A separate but related group of islands in the same body of water.

ash. Powdery residue produced in abundance by explosive volcanic eruptions.

botanist. A scientist who specializes in studying plants.

chemist. A scientist who specializes in studying matter, its components, and its properties.

cinder. Small, rough particles of hardened lava often produced in abundance during volcanic eruptions.

cone. The hill of extruded ash, cinder, and rock that piles up around a volcanic vent.

dinghies. Inflatable rubber boats; the singular is *dinghy*.

ecosystem. A community of living and nonliving things that are linked by their proximity to one another and, as a result, are interdependent.

entomologist. A scientist who specializes in studying insects.

excrement. Waste matter produced by animals; in other words: poop.

formaldehyde. A naturally occurring chemical often used to preserve dead insects; in the presence of formaldehyde, the insects will not decompose.

geologist. A scientist who specializes in studying the earth.

geyser. A geologic feature in which water heated underground intermittently boils over, sending a column of water and steam into the air.

lava. The extremely hot, semifluid rock that usually flows under the surface of the earth but is forced out during a volcanic eruption; the term can also refer to the same substance after it has cooled and formed a hard, rocklike substance (see *a'a lava* and *pahoehoe lava*).

lava bombs. Blobs of molten lava extruded during a volcanic eruption; they cool into solid rocks before reaching the ground.

magma. Essentially molten lava, except that magma flows underneath the earth's crust instead of on top of it.

microenvironment. The small area around an organism; this small area can have very different conditions from the larger environment.

molten lava. Extremely hot, liquefied rock forced out from beneath the earth's crust, usually during a volcanic eruption.

pahoehoe lava (pronounced: pa-HOY-HOY). When molten lava cools and hardens, it can take on a variety of shapes, textures, and colors, depending on its composition and on environmental conditions; pahoehoe lava hardens with a bumpy surface that is caused when this slow-moving lava begins to harden over irregularities in the surface it flows over.

palagonite tuff. The type of rock that forms when volcanic tephra is heated over time.

pioneer species. Species that are well suited to growing in newly disturbed or, in the case of Surtsey, newly formed places.

plume. A long or tall cloud of smoke that spreads out in a way that resembles a bird's feather, which is also called a plume.

pumice. A lightweight and gas-filled rock produced during a volcanic eruption.

simple community. Organisms living and interacting in a common location.

skerry. A small rocky island, usually considered too small for human habitation.

soil chemist. A scientist who specializes in the components of soil and their properties.

succession. The stepwise arrival of organisms to a new or disturbed location and their subsequent assembly into cooperative communities.

sweep net. A net attached to a long handle for ease of "sweeping" it through grassy habitats, usually in search of insects and other invertebrates.

tephra. Magma that bursts out of a volcano in solid chunks; it consists of tiny bits of ash, lightweight gas-filled pumice, or solid rocks and boulders.

For More Information

Read

Lasky, Kathryn, and Christopher G. Knight. *Surtsey: The Newest Place on Earth*. New York: Hyperion, 1992.

McMillan, Bruce. *Nights of the Pufflings*. Boston: Houghton Mifflin, 1995.

Rusch, Elizabeth, and Tom Uhlman. *Eruption! Volcanoes and the Science of Saving Lives*. Boston: Houghton Mifflin Harcourt, 2013.

Stewart, Melissa. *Classification of Life*. Minneapolis: Twenty-First Century Books, 2008.

Winchester, Simon. *When the Earth Shakes: Earthquakes, Volcanoes, and Tsunamis*. New York: Viking, 2015.

Watch

Surtsey: The Black Island. By Helga Brekkan and Tourney Nordin, Seylan Film Production, 2003.

Explore

The Surtsey Research Society
www.surtsey.is/index_eng.htm

National Geographic's Iceland Page
kids.nationalgeographic.com/explore/countries/iceland/#iceland-glacier.jpg

Iceland's Iceland Page
www.iceland.is

You can use an Internet search engine to find new information on the islands of Surtsey, Krakatoa, Anak Krakatoa, and, most especially, the currently growing island of Nishinoshima and the shrinking, unnamed new island in Tonga.

Source Notes

1. Arrival

"When darkness . . .": Thorarinsson, "Surtsey: Island Born of Fire," 715.

"Those of us who witnessed . . .": Thorarinsson, *Surtsey: The New Island*, 24.

"everyone got a ducking": Thorarinsson, "Surtsey: Island Born of Fire," 723.

"Hardly were we ashore . . .": Ibid.

"A volcanic island . . .": Ibid., 726.

"There were cracking noises . . .": Fridriksson, *Surtsey: Ecosystems Formed*, 8.

"It was not advisable . . .": Ibid.

2. Life

"greatest, wildest . . .": Winchester, *When the Earth Shakes*, 25.

"The first visitation . . .": Osmundson, "New Island Offers a Rich Field of Study," E7.

3. Growth

"Most invertebrate species . . .": Olafsson and Ingimarsdottir, "The Land-Invertebrate Fauna on Surtsey," 122.

4. Survival

"The colonizers were . . .": Fridriksson, *Surtsey: Ecosystems Formed*, 75.

All other quotations were taken from interviews conducted by the author on Surtsey during the week of July 13–17, 2015, or from follow-up email correspondence.

Selected Bibliography

Blanchard, Duncan. *From Raindrops to Volcanoes: Adventures with Sea Surface Meteorology.* New York: Anchor Books, 1967.

Fridriksson, Sturla. *Surtsey: Ecosystems Formed.* Reykjavik: The Surtsey Research Society, 2005.

Gudmundsson, Finnur. "Ornithological Work on Surtsey in 1969 and 1970." *Surtsey Research* 6 (1972): 64–65.

Magnússon, B., S. Magnússon, E. Olafsson, and B. Sigurdsson. "Plant Colonization, Succession and Ecosystem Development on Surtsey with Reference to Neighbouring Islands." *Biogeosciences* 11 (2014): 5521–37.

New, Tim R. "Colonization, Succession and Conservation: The Invertebrates of Anak Krakatau, Indonesia, and Contrast with Surtsey." *Surtsey Research* 13 (2015): 31–39.

"New Island May Solve Scientific Problems." *Irish Times,* June 22, 1965, 6.

Olafsson, Erling. "The Development of the Land-Arthropod Fauna on Surtsey, Iceland, During 1971–1976 with Notes on Terrestrial Oligochaeta." *Surtsey Research* 8 (1978): 41–46.

———. "The Status of Land-Arthropod Fauna on Surtsey, Iceland, in Summer 1981." *Surtsey Research* 9 (1982): 68–72.

Olafsson, Erling, and Lovisa Asbjornsdottir. *Surtsey In Focus.* Iceland: Edda Publishing, 2014.

Olafsson, Erling, and Maria Ingimarsdottir. "The Land-Invertebrate Fauna on Surtsey During 2002–2006." *Surtsey Research* 12 (2009): 113–28.

Osmundsen, John A. "New Island Offers a Rich Field of Study." *New York Times,* June 20, 1965, E7.

Porleifur, Einarsson. *The Surtsey Eruption in Words and Pictures.* Reykjavik: Heimskringla, 1965.

Sigmundsdottir, Alda. *The Little Book of Icelandic.* Reykjavik: Enska textasmidjan, 2016.

Thorarinsson, Sigurdur. *Surtsey: The New Island in the North Atlantic.* New York: Viking, 1967.

———. "Surtsey: Island Born of Fire." *National Geographic* 127, no. 5 (May 1965): 713–26.

Winchester, Simon. *When the Earth Shakes: Earthquakes, Volcanoes, and Tsunamis.* New York: Viking, 2015.

Acknowledgments

Thank you to Gerry Burns, who first took me to Iceland and who managed life at home when I had the opportunity to go back on my own. Thank you to the brilliant tour guide on Heimaey, who first pointed my gaze toward Surtsey and its scientists. Thank you to Borgþór Magnússon, who invited me to join the 2015 Surtsey expedition, and to Matthías Svavar Alfreðsson, Lovísa Ásbjörnsdóttir, Paweł Wąsowicz, Sigurður Magnússon, Bjarni Sigurðsson, Kristján Jónasson, and Þórdís Vilhelmina Bragadóttir for inviting me into the many stories playing out on this special island. Thank you to mycologist Guðríður Gyða Eyjólfsdóttir for help with mushroom identification, and thank you to Chris Raine, for setting me straight when I got cold feet about the North Atlantic. Thank you to my friend and editor, Erica Zappy Wainer, and the entire team at HMH Books for Young Readers, for supporting my vision and for helping me share it with readers. Most especially, and with endless admiration and gratitude, thank you to Erling Ólafsson, for sharing his work on Surtsey with me. This book owes much of its life to him.

Photo Credits

Matthías Alfreðsson: 69

Lovísa Àsbjörnsdóttir: 67, 68

Sigurjón Einarsson/Icelandic Institute of Natural History: 3, 5, 6

Sigurgeir Jónasson: 4

Borgþór Magnússon: 13

National Land Survey of Iceland and Icelandic Institute of Natural History: 7

Erling Ólafsson: 1, 8, 9, 11, 12, 15, 16, 17 (top, left and right), 18, 29 (top), 30, 33, 34, 38, 39, 40 (right), 41, 42, 44, 48 (top), 55 (right), 60 (top), 65

Paweł Wąsowicz: 21, 31

All other photos by Loree Griffin Burns

Index

Note: Page references in **bold** indicate photo or illustration captions.